Dream BIG American Idol SUPERSTARS

American Idol Profiles Index: Top Finalists from Seasons 1 to 7 (82 Contestants)

Chuck Bednar

Mason Crest Publishers

Produced by 21st Century Publishing and Communications, Inc.

MASON CREST PUBLISHERS INC.
370 Reed Road
Broomall, Pennsylvania 19008
(866) MCP-BOOK (toll free)
www.masoncrest.com

Printed in the United States of America.

First Printing

9 8 7 6 5 4 3 2 1

Library of Congress Cataloging-in-Publication Data

Bednar, Chuck, 1976–
    American idol profiles index : top finalists from each season (82 contestants) / Chuck Bednar.
        p. cm. — (Dream big: American idol superstars)
    Includes index.
    ISBN 978-1-4222-1516-6 (hardback : alk. paper)
    ISBN 978-1-4222-1593-7 (pbk. : alk. paper)
    1. American idol (Television program)—Juvenile literature. 2. Popular music—
Competitions—United States—Juvenile literature. 3. Singers—United States—
Juvenile literature. I. Title.
    ML76.A54B43 2010
    782.42164092'273—dc22
    [B]   2009022765

Publisher's notes:
    All quotations in this book come from original sources, and contain the spelling and
    grammatical inconsistencies of the original text.

    The Web sites mentioned in this book were active at the time of publication. The publisher
    is not responsible for Web sites that have changed their addresses or discontinued
    operation since the date of publication. The publisher will review and update the
    Web site addresses each time the book is reprinted.

    American Idol ® is a registered trademark of 19 TV Ltd. and FremantleMedia
    North America, Inc.

CONTENTS

American Idol TIMELINE

October 5, 2001

Pop Idol, a TV reality show created by Simon Fuller, debuts in the United Kingdom and becomes a smash hit.

January 21, 2003

American Idol Season 2 premieres without Brian Dunkleman, leaving Ryan Seacrest as the sole host.

Fall 2001

Based on the success of *Pop Idol*, and after initially rejecting the concept, FOX Network agrees to buy *American Idol*, a national talent competition and TV reality show.

May 21, 2003

- *American Idol* Season 2 finale airs.
- Ruben Studdard narrowly wins and Clay Aiken is the runner-up.
- Runner-up Clay Aiken goes on to become extremely successful both critically and commercially.

Spring 2002

Auditions for *American Idol* Season 1 are held in New York City, Los Angeles, Chicago, Dallas, Miami, Atlanta, and Seattle.

January 19, 2004

American Idol Season 3 premieres.

2001   2002   2003   2004

June 11, 2002

American Idol Season 1 premieres on FOX Network, with Simon Cowell, Paula Abdul, and Randy Jackson as the judges, and Ryan Seacrest and Brian Dunkleman as the co-hosts.

January 27, 2004

William Hung's audition is aired and his humble response to Simon Cowell's scathing criticism make William the most famous American Idol non-qualifier and earn him record deals and a cult-like following.

September 4, 2002

- *American Idol* Season 1 finale airs.
- Kelly Clarkson wins and Justin Guarini is the runner-up.
- Kelly Clarkson goes on to become the most successful Idol winner and a superstar in the musical industry.

April 21, 2004

Jennifer Hudson is voted off the show in 7th place, and goes on to win the role of Effie in *Dreamgirls*, for which she wins an Academy Award, a Golden Globe Award, and a Grammy Award.

Fall 2002

Auditions for *American Idol* Season 2 are held in New York City, Los Angeles, Miami, Detroit, Nashville, and Austin.

May 26, 2004

- *American Idol* Season 3 finale airs with 65 million viewers casting their votes.
- Fantasia Barrino is crowned the winner and Diana DeGarmo is the runner-up.
- Fantasia soon becomes the first artist in the history of Billboard to debut at number one with her first single.

May 10, 2006

Chris Daughtry is voted off the show in 4th place, and soon after forms the band, Daughtry, and releases its debut album, which becomes number one on the charts, wins many awards, and finds huge commercial success.

April 26, 2006

Kellie Pickler is voted off the show in 6th place, and soon releases her debut album, which rockets to number one on the Billboard Top Country Album chart.

January 17, 2006

American Idol Season 5 premieres and for the first time airs in high definition.

May 24, 2006

- *American Idol* Season 5 finale airs.
- Taylor Hicks is the winner and Katharine McPhee the runner-up.
- Elliot Yamin, the second runner-up, goes on to release his debut album, which goes gold.

January 16, 2007

American Idol Season 6 premieres.

April 2007

The *American Idol* Songwriting Contest is announced.

January 15, 2008

American Idol Season 7 airs with a four-hour two-day premiere.

April 9, 2008

Idol Gives Back returns for its second year.

May 21, 2008

- *American Idol* Season 7 finale airs.
- David Cook wins with 54.6 million votes and David Archuleta is the runner-up with 42.9 million votes.
- Both Davids go on to tremendous post-Idol success with successful albums and singles.

2005   2006   2007   2008   2009

May 25, 2005

- *American Idol* Season 4 finale airs.
- Carrie Underwood wins and Bo Bice is the runner-up.
- Carrie goes on to become one of the most successful Idol winners, selling millions of albums and winning scores of major awards.

January 18, 2005

- *American Idol* Season 4 premieres.
- Some rules change:
  - The age limit is raised from 24 to 28.
  - The semi-final competition is separated by gender up until the 12 finalists.

April 24–25, 2007

American Idol Gives Back, a charitable campaign to raise money for underprivileged children worldwide, airs, and raises more than $70 million.

May 23, 2007

- *American Idol* Season 6 finale airs.
- Jordin Sparks wins with 74 million votes and Blake Lewis is the runner-up.
- Jordin goes on to join Kelly Clarkson and Carrie Underwood in the ranks of highly successful post-Idol recording artists.

January 13, 2009

American Idol Season 8 premieres adding Kara DioGuardi as a fourth judge.

February 14, 2009

The American Idol Experience, a theme park attraction, officially opens at Disney's Hollywood Studio in Florida.

May 20, 2009

- *American Idol* Season 8 finale airs.
- Kris Allen unexpectedly wins and Adam Lambert is the runner-up.
- Almost 100 million people voted in the season 8 finale.

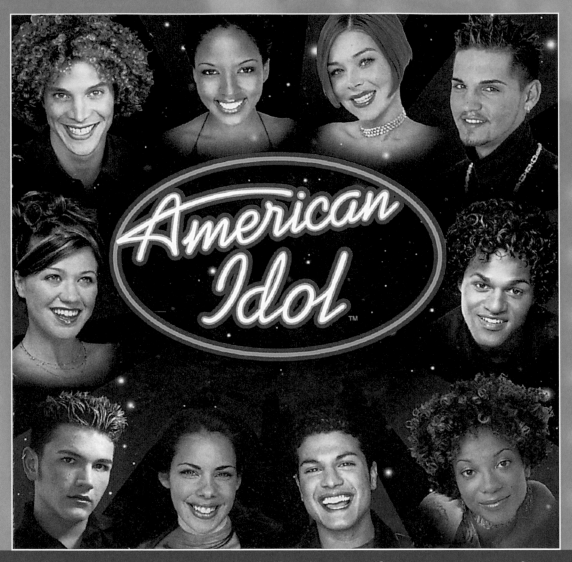

The first *American Idol* auditions were held in the spring of 2002. Contestants who passed the initial audition performed for judges Simon Cowell, Paula Abdul, and Randy Jackson. Those who advanced were sent to Hollywood, where 30 semifinalists were chosen and randomly split into three groups. The top three from each group made it into the finals, along with lone Wild Card R.J. Helton, who was chosen to make up the final 10. Season one was co-hosted by Ryan Seacrest and Brian Dunkleman, with Brian leaving the show after this season.

American Idol
Season

Despite its origins as a spinoff from a British TV show, *American Idol* has evolved into more than just something people watch on television. It has become the ultimate opportunity to make—or even become—the next big star in the world of music. Anyone with enough talent and big enough dreams can audition for the show, be featured on national television, and maybe even land a major recording contract and tens of millions of fans in the process. As Alan LeStourgeon of the American Idol News Web site puts it,

"American Idol is a phenom because unlike all the other talent shows that have ever been on TV, it delivers to America part of a dream millions have of being famous. . . . American Idol is what it is because it is the American Dream."

American Idol was created by manager and producer Simon Fuller, who had already created the hit program *Pop Idol* in England. For eight seasons and more than 300 episodes, the show has captured the imagination of both fans and dreamers everywhere. Each year, auditions are held in cities all over the United States. From the more than 10,000 people who audition each year, judges Simon Cowell, Randy Jackson, Paula Abdul, and Kara DioGuardi (who was added in season eight) select a group of semifinalists.

The semifinalists fly to Hollywood and complete in a series of performances on a live TV broadcast. The judges then rate their efforts, but viewers have the final say by voting for their favorites via telephone or text message. The next day, the results are announced, and the person who receives the fewest votes from the public is typically eliminated. Eventually, two will remain, competing head-to-head with both the title of American Idol and a record deal at stake.

Season 1

The show, which was originally entitled *American Idol: The Search for a Superstar*, premiered on June 11, 2002. The 25 first episodes averaged approximately 10 million viewers each. By the end of the season, however, the audience grew immensely, with more than 22 million people tuned in for the September 4 season finale.

The first season of *American Idol* featured 10 finalists who started competing against each other in themed performance nights, such as Motown, 1960s, and Big Band, starting in July. The finals pitted Kelly Clarkson against Justin Guarini, with Kelly winning on the strength of her song "A Moment Like This," as well as her cover version of Aretha Franklin's "Respect."

#1

Kelly Brianne Clarkson was born in Burleson, Texas, and raised in nearby Fort Worth. The youngest of three children, she was born on April 24, 1982, and her singing talent was discovered by a junior high school teacher. While on *American Idol,* she performed several songs from Motown great Aretha Franklin, including "Respect" and "Natural Woman."

On September 4, 2002, Kelly became the first person to win *American Idol,* earning 58 percent of the fan vote. She won a recording contract with RCA Records, and has made good use of it. She has released four albums, including 2009's *All I Ever Wanted,* which debuted at number one on the *Billboard* 200. Kelly has sold more than 20 million albums worldwide during her career, and she is a two-time Grammy Award winner as well.

#2

Justin Guarini was born Justin Eldrin Bell on October 28, 1978. He was born in Columbus, Georgia, but moved to Doylestown, Pennsylvania and took his stepfather's name when his mother remarried. During auditions, he was deemed a favorite when the quality of his voice earned rare praise from Simon. However, he wound up finishing as runner-up.

Even so, RCA signed him to a record deal. In June 2003, he released his self-titled debut album, which peaked at number 20 on the *Billboard* Hot 200. Since then, Justin has parted ways with RCA, but he went on to release a second album and is currently working on a third. He also co-hosts the TV Guide Network shows *Idol Wrap* and *Idol Tonight,* and in February 2009, announced plans to marry high school sweetheart Reina Capodici.

#3

Katherine Nicole "Nikki" McKibbin was born in Grand Prairie, Texas, on September 28, 1978. Before competing on *American Idol,* Nikki appeared on the TV show *Popstars* and ran a karaoke production company. Her best performance on the show came on July 24, 2002, when she belted out a powerful version of the Janis Joplin hit "Piece of My Heart." She was eliminated in third place on August 28, 2002.

Nikki signed with RCA Records but later left because she was unwilling to do a country music album. Instead, her first CD, *Unleashed,* came in 2005 with the Dallas-based heavy metal band Downside. As she told *USA Today,* "I'd rather be broke and happy than rich and miserable." Nikki would later appear on multiple reality shows, and is currently raising a family in Fort Worth, Texas.

#4

Tamyra Monica Gray was born in Takoma Park, Maryland, on July 26, 1979, and grew up in Norcross, Georgia. Tamyra attended Georgia State University, worked a variety of jobs, and appeared in a few commercials prior to *American Idol.* While she finished fourth and was voted off on August 21, 2002, Simon said her performance of "A House is Not a Home" was "one of the best performances on television."

Tamyra's first solo CD, *The Dreamer,* was released by 19 Records in May 2004. Since then she has parted ways with the label and has pursued an acting career. Tamyra was a semi-regular on the ABC TV show *Boston Legal,* had a supporting role in the film *The Gospel,* and was a member of the cast of the Broadway show *Rent* in 2007 and 2008. She is married to Color Me Badd singer Sam Watters.

#5

Richard Jason "R.J." Helton was born on May 17, 1981, in Pasadena, Texas, but later moved to Cumming, Georgia. He became one of the first season finalists via the Wild Card round by singing "Lately" by Stevie Wonder. R.J. made it to the final five, but on August 14, 2002, he became the first of that quintet to be eliminated.

After *American Idol*, R.J. hooked up with manager Mathew Knowles (the father of pop icon Beyoncé) and released *Real Life*, a collection of contemporary Christian songs, in 2004. He has appeared on *The Tonight Show with Jay Leno*, *The Today Show*, *Good Morning America*, and *Total Request Live*. In early 2009, he was performing at various locations in Nevada, and had also started work on both a second CD and an autobiography.

#6

Christina Christian was born on June 21, 1981, in Brooklyn, New York. During her time on *American Idol*, she sang "At Last" by Etta James and "Ain't No Mountain High Enough" by Marvin Gaye and Tammi Terrell. Her final performance was "The Glory of Love" by Peggy Lee, and afterwards she was hospitalized for exhaustion as fans voted her off in sixth place on August 7, 2002.

Christina signed a record deal with 19 Entertainment in late 2002, but has yet to release her first solo CD. In 2003, she appeared as a guest star on the hit CBS television show *CSI: Crime Scene Investigation*, and secured a role as a correspondent on the TV Guide Network. Christina married Nicholas Cewe in 2004, and two years later, she became a mother with the birth of her son.

#7

Ryan Starr was born Tiffany Ryan Montgomery on November 21, 1982 in Sunland, California. As a child, she was influenced by Etta James, Ella Fitzgerald, Billy Holiday, and Janis Joplin. She was mentored by Paula Abdul during her time on *American Idol,* and garnered praise for her performance of Stevie Wonder's "If You Really Love Me." On July 31, 2002, she was voted off the show, finishing seventh.

She was initially signed by RCA following the show, but never recorded an album for them and was released from her contract in 2005. Later on that year, her song "My Religion" was released via iTunes and became the most downloaded song in the service's history. Ryan has done some acting, appearing on both *CSI* and *That '70s Show,* and often works with abused and underprivileged children in Los Angeles.

#8

Abner Juda "A.J." Gil was born in San Diego, California, on July 5, 1984. He is of Mexican-American descent and, as one of 10 children, endured many tough times growing up. His trademark songs on *American Idol* came during Motown Week, when he performed "My Cherie Amour" by Stevie Wonder. On July 24, 2002, he was eliminated in eighth place.

A.J. joined other *American Idol* finalists for the 2002 world tour, then moved to L.A. and underwent training in audio engineering. In 2009, he starred as Chris in the direct-to-DVD motion picture *Destination Fame.* On April 12, 2009, A.J. performed as part of the "Sunday Sessions" R&B show in Reseda, California. He is single, currently working on his debut CD, and recruiting musicians through his Web site to work alongside him.

#9

Jim Verraros of Crystal Lake, Illinois, was born on February 8, 1983. He was raised by deaf parents, and thus is quite proficient in American Sign Language. Even as a child, he had a gift for music, which he put on display during his performance of the hit Commodores song "Easy" during his time on *American Idol.* Even so, on July 17, 2002, Jim was the second finalist eliminated.

Jim released his independent, award-winning CD *Unsaid and Understood* in 2004, and Koch Records handled his first mainstream release, *Rollercoster,* in 2005. His song "You Turn It On" became a top 10 single on *Billboard*'s dance charts. He currently lives in Chicago and has appeared in several independent motion pictures. Jim's third CD, *Do Not Disturb,* is due out sometime in 2009.

#10

Earl James "EJay" Day was born on September 13, 1981, in Lawrenceville, Georgia. In the semifinals, Jay performed "I'll Be" and "My Girl," earning his way into the final round. He was also the first finalist to be voted off, though, exiting in tenth place on July 17, 2002.

Afterwards, he joined other *American Idol* performers on a concert tour. He continues to perform, and has even appeared at several events at the request of boxing legend Muhammad Ali. EJay also wrote the song "Pure Love" for Raven-Symoné's second CD, *Undeniable.* In 2003, he appeared at the Tournament of Roses Parade in Pasadena, California, and in 2005, he signed to perform with Royal Caribbean cruise ships. As he told *People* magazine, "it's a good job while I'm trying to make it in the business."

Season two began with auditions in the fall of 2002. Among the 32 semifinalists were four Wild Cards: Kimberly Caldwell (chosen by Randy), Trenyce (by Paula), Carmen Rasmussen (by Simon), and Clay Aiken (by public vote). Clay went on the become the first *Idol* Wild Card nonwinner to enjoy a very successful post-*Idol* career, selling five million albums, more than any other male singer in *Idol* history. His debut album, *Measure of a Man*, opened at number 1 with first week sales of 613,000 copies, a record for the biggest weekly album sales of any Idol.

American Idol
Season

The ratings growth during the end of season one led the Fox television network to move up the start of the second season to January 2003. Two additional finalists were added, bringing the total to 12, and the number of episodes increased from 25 in the first season to 38 for the second. The ratings nearly tripled from season one, with an average of 26.5 million people watching each week. In season two Ruben Studdard edged out Clay Aiken in a controversial finale that saw phone lines flooded and millions of calls reportedly dropped.

#1

Christopher Ruben Studdard was born in Frankfurt, Germany, on September 12, 1978, and was raised in Birmingham, Alabama. He sang gospel at his local Baptist church and played football in high school—even earning a scholarship to Alabama A&M University. Eager to pursue a career in music, Ruben was part of a jazz band before winning *American Idol* on May 21, 2003.

The anticipation for his first album, *Soulful,* led to more than a million preorders for the December 2003 release, which debuted at number one on the *Billboard* 200. *Soulful* helped the "Velvet Teddy Bear" earn a Grammy Award nomination and win the 2004 NAACP Image Award for Outstanding New Artist. Ruben since has lost over 70 pounds and released three additional CDs, including the most recent, *Love IS,* in May 2009.

#2

Clay Aiken was born Clayton Holmes Grissom on November 30, 1978, in Raleigh, North Carolina. Prior to *American Idol,* he performed with bands and choirs, acted in musicals, and even cut three demo CDs. Clay became one of the second season's breakout stars, leading the fan voting each week—until the May 21, 2003 finale, when he was edged out by Ruben Studdard and finished as the runner-up.

Clay's debut CD, *Measure of a Man,* was released in October 2003 and went on to sell three million copies. He also won the Fans Choice Award at the 2003 American Music Awards. Since then, Clay has released four additional albums, written a bestselling book, and made his Broadway debut in *Monty Python's Spamalot.* In 2005, he was voted the most-loved reality TV star of all time by the readers of *TV Guide.*

#3

Kimberley Dawn Locke was born in Hartsville, Tennessee, on January 3, 1978. She graduated from Belmont University and traveled to Nashville to try out for *American Idol* on October 30, 2002. She sang "Over the Rainbow" at the auditions and during the semifinal round, making it into the final three before being eliminated on May 14, 2003.

In September 2003, she signed a contract with Curb Records and released her first CD, *One Love,* on May 4, 2004. With her single "8th World Wonder," Kimberley became the first *American Idol* performer to have a number-one hit with a song that was not performed on the show. Her second album, *Based on a True Story,* was released in May 2007. Kimberley is also currently enjoying a successful career as a plus-sized model.

#4

Joshua Mario "Josh" Gracin was born on October 18, 1980, in Westland, Michigan. At the age of 16, he performed in a talent show at the Grand Ole Opry, and later attended Western Michigan University before joining the Marines. He was eliminated from *American Idol* on May 7, 2003, finishing in fourth position.

Following his time on the show, Josh completed his service to the Marine Corps and was honorably discharged in September 2004. He also released his self-titled debut CD in 2004. *Josh Gracin* featured three *Billboard* top-five country songs, including the number one hit "Nothin' to Lose." His second album, *We Weren't Crazy,* followed in March 2009, and a third is expected sometime in 2009. He and his wife Anne Marie currently live in Nashville, Tennessee, where they raise their four children.

#5

Trenyce was born Lashundra Trenyce Cobbins on March 31, 1980, in Memphis, Tennessee. A naturally gifted musician, Trenyce received a full music scholarship to the University of Memphis, where she studied nursing before deciding to devote herself to performing. She was selected as a semifinalist, and her performance of "Let's Stay Together" earned her a spot in the finals. Trenyce was eliminated on April 30, 2003, finishing fifth.

While she toured along with fellow *American Idol* alumni immediately following the show and performed throughout Russia in 2006, Trenyce has yet to record her debut album. She founded a performing arts school in her hometown of Memphis. Trenyce has also become active in musical theater, starring in stage productions of *Dreamgirls, Not a Day Goes By, Love in the Nick of Tyme,* and most recently, *Ain't Misbehavin'* alongside Ruben Studdard.

#6

Carmen Rasmussen was born on March 25, 1985, in Edmonton, Alberta, Canada. She was still a high school senior when she auditioned for *American Idol*, making the cut thanks to her performance of "Can't Fight the Moonlight" during the Wild Card round. During the show, she had to spend three hours per day with a tutor. Carmen was eliminated in sixth place on April 23, 2003.

Later on that year, she made her acting debut in a remake of *Pride & Prejudice,* and in 2004, she released an EP entitled *Carmen* on the R3 Records label. The following year, Carmen married Bradley Herbert. Then in 2007, she released her country music CD *Nothin' Like the Summer* and saw her book *Staying In Tune* published. Carmen gave birth to a baby boy named Boston in January 2009.

#7

Kimberly Ann Caldwell was born on February 25, 1982, in Katy, Texas. Even before *American Idol*, she had made a name for herself musically. She had been a multi-time winner on *Star Search* and in 1995, she performed during the 50th wedding anniversary celebration of former President George H.W. Bush and his wife Barbara. She finished seventh and was voted off on April 16, 2003.

Kimberly has since become a well-known television personality. She covers *American Idol* and various awards ceremonies for TV Guide Network and hosts both the CBS game show *Jingles* and the MTV reality series *P. Diddy's StarMaker*. She has also appeared in the movies *Wrong Turn 2: Dead End* and *Memories of Murder*. Kimberly is currently working on her first CD, and in 2008 released a pair of singles via the iTunes download service.

#8

Richard Eugene "Rickey" Smith was born on May 10, 1979, in Keene, Texas. Before *American Idol*, Rickey had been trained as an opera singer and competed in many different talent shows and competitions. His semifinal performance of "One Last Cry" by Brian McKnight propelled him into the final 12, but on April 9, 2003, he became the fifth performer to be eliminated.

USA Today caught up with Rickey in May 2008. At that time, he had moved to Oklahoma City, Oklahoma, and had taken a bartending job at a local sports bar. Rickey told reporter Andrew McGinn that he felt like he was close to a record deal. However, financial troubles forced him to put his musical dreams on hold indefinitely. Rickey called his post-*Idol* struggles "frustrating" but added that he's "made peace with it."

#9

Corey Delaney Clark was born in San Bernardino, California, on July 13, 1980. At the age of 13, he was hired on as a backup singer for Barry Manilow for a week-long concert series in Las Vegas. Corey was one of the second season finalists before being disqualified from *American Idol* on April 2, 2003, for allegedly lying about his arrest record (an accusation he has repeatedly denied).

Corey released his self-titled debut album on June 21, 2005. Unfortunately, since then he has found himself in frequent legal trouble. In July 2005, he was charged with battery following an incident at a hotel. Later on, Corey's wife took out a restraining order against him (the two have since separated), he was placed on probation for harassing his father-in-law, and he was arrested for possession of a controlled substance.

#10

Julia Megan DeMato was born on March 7, 1979, in Brookfield, Connecticut. On *American Idol*, she performed "Son of a Preacher Man" by Dusty Springfield and "Breathe" by Faith Hill, among other songs. She was voted off the show on March 26, 2003, and finished in tenth place.

Following her time on the show, Julia recorded a cover of "At Last" for the *American Idol 2 Love Songs* CD. She briefly worked as the host of *Meow TV* on the Oxygen network, and recorded a song called "Let It Rain" that was digitally distributed. In December 2005, Julia was arrested and charged with DUI. She pleaded guilty and was sentenced to rehab and community service. Julia currently lives in Brookfield, works as a cosmetologist, and at last word was engaged to an electrician named Jim Polches.

#11 **Charles William Grigsby, Jr.** was born on September 15, 1978. While he had no formal training as a child, music became so important to this Oberlin, Ohio, native that he dropped out of school to pursue a career in music. During the *American Idol* semifinals, despite suffering from the stomach flu, he delivered an inspirational performance of Stevie Wonder's "Overjoyed" and became one of the season's 12 finalists.

However, Charles was eliminated in 11th position on March 19, 2003. He went on to become a folk hero in his home state. In July 2005, CitiBoyz Music released his first CD, a self-titled collection of six songs. Later that year, he embarked on a promotional tour for his CD. Starting in 2006, Charles took time off and returned home after losing a cousin to diabetes.

#12 **Vanessa Denae Olivarez** was born in Atlanta, Georgia, on February 3, 1981. Before appearing on the show, she worked at a salon and trained at the Gwinnett School of Fine Arts. Vanessa made it to Hollywood by performing Queen's "Bohemian Rhapsody," but she was the first finalist eliminated as she was voted off on March 12, 2003.

After *American Idol,* Vanessa signed with Toronto, Ontario, Canada–based Outta the Box Records. Her first single, "The One," reached the ninth position on Canadian sales charts. In 2004, she starred in a Toronto production of the musical *Hairspray,* and earned a Dora Award nomination for Outstanding Performance by a Female in a Principal Role–Musical. In 2006, she returned to Atlanta and released an EP with the blues rock band Butterfly Stitch. They are currently working on a studio album.

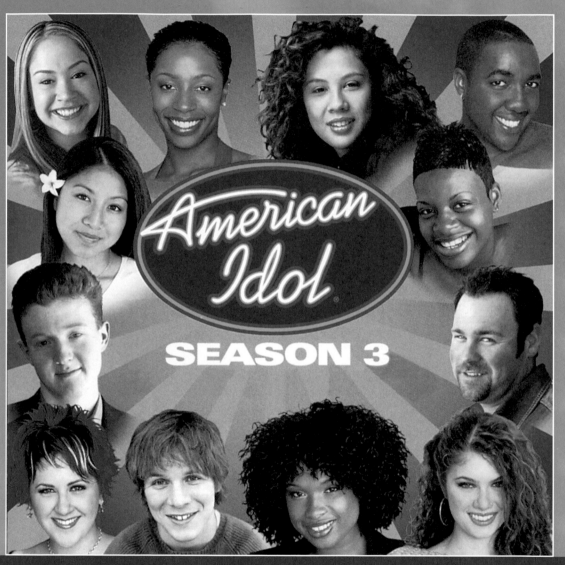

The success of the *American Idol* continued into season three, which earned the Fox network more than $260 million that year. Eight of the 12 finalists were female, and the season was the only one so far where both the winner and the runner-up were women. The most successful contestant—winner or not—was Jennifer Hudson, who went on to win Oscar and Grammy awards.

American Idol
Season

3

Season three of *American Idol* debuted on January 19, 2004, and while Fantasia Barrino was crowned the winner, she was just one of the many stars who emerged during the year. One of the first was William Hung, a University of California, Berkeley student who performed a famously bad version of Ricky Martin's "She Bangs" during auditions. William became a cult favorite among viewers, and despite his vocal shortcomings, managed to secure a record deal. More than 350 million total viewers tuned during the season, including nearly 29 million for the May 26 season finale.

#1 Fantasia Monique Barrino

was born June 30, 1984, in High Point, North Carolina. A single mother who had endured a difficult life prior to the *American Idol* auditions, she quickly became a star. Randy Jackson called her performance of "Summertime" the best in *American Idol* history. On May 26, 2004, she defeated runner-up Diana DeGarmo by more than a million votes and became the third season champion.

Just days after the *Idol* finale, Fantasia released "I Believe" and became the first artist to ever top the *Billboard* Hot 100 with a debut single. Her first CD, *Free Yourself*, came out in November 2004. In March 2005, Fantasia won the NAACP Image Award for Outstanding Female Artist, and in September, her bestselling book *Life is Not a Fairy Tale* was published. She is currently working on her third album.

#2 Diana Nicole DeGarmo

was born on June 16, 1987, in Birmingham, Alabama. She was an experienced performer prior to auditioning for *American Idol*, having worked in various theater productions as a kid, winning the 2002 Miss Teen Georgia pageant, and making it to the finals of *American's Most Talented Kid*. She made it all the way to the May 26, 2004, finale, where she finished in second place.

Her first single, "Dreams," was released on June 24, 2004, and her debut album, *Blue Skies*, followed on December 7. In December 2005, she embarked on a USO tour, and in 2006 made her Broadway debut in *Hairspray*. She recently released a four-song EP called *Unplugged in Nashville*, and is currently working on a country music CD that should be released sometime in 2009.

#3

Jasmine Soriano Trias was born in Honolulu, Hawaii, on November 3, 1986. At age eight, she enrolled in the Performing Artist Academy, and shortly thereafter the Filipino singer began winning statewide talent competitions. On *American Idol,* Jasmine became a worldwide sensation, and with the help of the international vote, made it into the final three. She was eliminated in third place on May 19, 2004.

In September 2004, Jasmine went to the Philippines, where she not only signed endorsement deals with McDonald's and several other companies, but also performed her first solo concert. Her first single, "Flying Home," was distributed exclusively at Pizza Hut and Taco Bell restaurants in Hawaii. In 2005, she released her self-titled first CD, which earned her a pair of Hawaii Music Awards. She is currently in L.A. working on a follow-up.

#4

La Toya Renee London was born in San Francisco, California, on December 29, 1978, and was a member of the Oakland Youth Chorus as a teenager. On *American Idol,* La Toya's renditions of "All By Myself," "Ooh Baby Baby," "Somewhere," and "All the Time" earned gushing praise from the judges. However, she was eliminated on May 12, 2004, and finished in fourth place overall.

Following her departure from the show, La Toya was immediately signed by Peak Records, and her debut CD *Love & Life* was released on September 20, 2005. In 2006, she began acting, joining the cast of the play *Issues: We All Have 'Em* in February and starring in the award-winning musical *Beehive* that summer. In 2007, La Toya took on the role of Nettie in *The Color Purple,* earning an NAACP Theater Award nomination for her performance.

#5

George Clayton Huff, Jr. was born in New Orleans, Louisiana, on November 4, 1980. George made the most of second chances during his time on *American Idol.* He was brought in as a replacement for a disqualified contestant. Then he was initially passed over, but later reached the finals through the Wild Card round. George was eliminated on May 5, 2004, and finished in fifth place.

His debut CD, *Miracles,* was released by Miracle Records on October 11, 2005. Shortly thereafter, he was forced to leave home and relocate to his brother's house in Dallas following Hurricane Katrina. He continued performing during that time, staging a 2006 concert at West Virginia University and following that up with a Christmas show in Salinas, California. George has since returned home and released his self-titled second CD in April 2009.

#6

John Bassat Stevens IV was born in Buffalo, New York, on July 28, 1987. This Dean Martin–style crooner performed "That's Amore" and "The Way You Look Tonight" on the show. John struggled with other musical styles, though, and was eliminated in sixth place on April 28, 2004. The 16-year-old was the youngest *American Idol* finalist to date.

Afterwards, John signed with Maverick Records and released his first album, *Red,* on June 28, 2005. *Red* debuted in the top ten of the *Billboard* jazz charts, but sales were modest. John eventually decided to step away from the business for a while and enter Boston's Berklee College of Music, where he studied performance, songwriting, and music business. The 2008-09 year was scheduled to be his last at the school, so expect John to resurface shortly.

#7

Jennifer Kate Hudson was born on September 12, 1981, in Chicago, Illinois. Inspired by Aretha Franklin, Whitney Houston, and Patti LaBelle, Jennifer found work singing on Disney Cruise Lines prior to her time on *American Idol.* Her performance of "Circle of Life" from *The Lion King* earned her the highest votes during top nine week. She was voted off on April 21, 2004, finishing in sixth place.

Despite finishing in the middle of the pack during *Idol*'s third season, Jennifer has gone on to become a major star. She won an Academy Award for her breakout performance in the 2006 film *Dreamgirls.* Jennifer has appeared in four movies, with a fifth, *Winged Creatures,* due out in 2009. She also released a self-titled CD in September 2008, and performed the national anthem at Super Bowl XLIII.

#8

Jon Peter Lewis, often referred to as just JPL, was born in Lincoln, Nebraska, on November 7, 1979. He reportedly cashed in his college loans to fly out to Honolulu for the *American Idol* auditions. Jon's performance of "A Little Less Conversation" earned him a whopping 22 percent of the votes during the Wild Card round, but ultimately he was bumped off in eighth place on April 15, 2004.

JPL released his first single, the blues-funk hybrid "Turn to Grey," shortly thereafter. His first CD, *Stories from Hollywood,* came out on his 27th birthday, in November 2006. Jon followed that up with a second album, *Break the Silence,* in July 2008. Monica Rizzo of *People* magazine called *Break the Silence* "one of the best pop/rock CDs of the year." He is currently on tour to support his sophomore release.

#9 Ciara-Camile Roque Velasco

was born on September 1, 1985, in the Philippines, but grew up in Maui, Hawaii. Before *American Idol*, she worked as a waitress at her family's IHOP restaurant. During auditions, her performance of the Fugees' "Ready or Not" prompted Randy Jackson to mention how he loved the "dark" quality of her voice. Camile also impressed in the semifinals, but was voted off in 9th place on April 7, 2004.

Camile traveled to the Philippines for a Christmas concert following her elimination. In 2005, she performed at the Pro Bowl Concert in Hawaii, and in February 2007, she opened for Lauryn Hill. In April 2008, she launched *CamileTV*, a series of weekly music-themed broadcasts created for YouTube. Her debut CD, *Koy*, was set to be released by Up Above Records in 2009.

#10 Amy Christina Adams

was born in Kansas City, Missouri, on July 25, 1979. Amy auditioned in Atlanta, Georgia, and joined the third group of semifinalists. Her most noteworthy performance on the show was a cover of the Dixie Chicks song "Sin Wagon," but she was eliminated on March 31, 2004, finishing in 10th place.

These days, family is Amy's primary focus. In May 2005, she gave birth to a son, Harrison. She, her husband Ryan, her son, and her stepdaughter currently live in Bakersfield, California. In 2005, she toured as part of the musical *Joseph and the Amazing Technicolor Dreamcoat*. She has expressed interest in doing future work on Broadway, and has also been working on a country music CD. She would also like to start a film career someday.

#11

Matthew Wyatt Rogers, who was born on September 16, 1978, in Rancho Cucamonga, California, isn't exactly your typical *American Idol* contestant. While he began singing at an early age, his biggest pre-*Idol* accomplishment was playing on the offensive line of the 2001 Rose Bowl champion Washington Huskies football team. He covered Otis Redding and Lonestar songs on the show but was the second person eliminated on March 24, 2004.

That summer, Matthew lost his mother to cancer. He went into television, working on *American Idol Extra, Turner Sports College Football,* and Fox Sports. Matthew is currently the host of the Discovery Channel show *Really Big Things* as well as the head football coach at Mission Viejo High School in California. He is also an avid card player with dreams of someday winning the World Series of Poker.

#12

Leah LaBelle Vladowski was born in Toronto, Ontario, Canada, on September 8, 1986. Leah was quite accomplished before her time on *American Idol.* In 1997, she won the Washington Pre-Teen Miss America Pageant. From 2000 to 2002, she starred in a children's reality TV show, and in 2002, she won a spot opening for the likes of Usher, Nelly, and LL Cool J during the Summer Jam 20 concert.

Leah finished 12th during season three of *American Idol* and was eliminated on March 17, 2004. Immediately afterwards, she returned to Seattle and completed high school. In October 2004, she joined other Pacific Northwest performers on a Christmas-themed charity album, and in 2005, she began recording material in an attempt to land a record deal. Leah moved to Boston and enrolled in the Berklee College of Music in September 2006.

Season four's age-limit increase gave two rockers, Bo Bice and Constantine Maroulis, the opportunity to compete in the show that had previously featured pop and R&B singers. The finale saw the battle between Bo and country singer Carrie Underwood, who was crowned the winner. Her phenomenon post-Idol success has inspired many to follow their dreams and helped the show become a real star-maker.

American Idol
Season

Prior to the fourth season, the show made some major changes. For starters, the maximum age of contestants was raised from 26 to 28, and semifinalists were grouped by gender to give both men and women equal opportunity. Also, while guest judges had previously been involved with the competition phase, they were used during auditions for the first time in 2005. The changes had a positive impact on the ratings, as an average of 33 million viewers watched each of the 45 episodes, which ran from January 18 through May 25.

#1

Carrie Marie Underwood was born on March 10, 1983, in Muskogee, Oklahoma. In 1996, she was close to signing with Capitol Records, but the deal fell through, and eventually her big break came on *American Idol.* During the March 22, 2005, episode, her rendition of Heart's "Alone" led Simon to predict she would win. He was right, as Carrie was crowned the fourth season winner on May 25.

Her debut CD, *Some Hearts,* was released on November 15, 2005, and became the best-selling debut for a female country artist in history. A second album, *Carnival Ride,* followed on October 23, 2007, and a third is due out in late 2009. Carrie has won more than 50 awards for her work thus far, including four Grammys, five American Music Awards, and eight Academy of Country Music Awards.

#2

Harold Elwin "Bo" Bice, Jr. was born in Huntsville, Alabama, on November 1, 1975. Prior to *American Idol,* Bo was a regular club performer and managed a guitar shop. Bo, 28, decided to audition after the age limit was raised. While he says he never expected to win, he came close, making it to the May 25, 2005, finale and finishing second.

In June 2005, Bo married Caroline Fisher, and in September, his son, Aidan, was born. On December 14, his debut album, *The Real Thing,* was released. Since then, Bo has been an active performer, despite medical issues that have forced him to undergo more than 20 surgeries. He and his work have been featured on numerous TV shows, films, and commercials, and his second CD, *See the Light,* came out on October 23, 2007.

#3

Vonzell Monique Solomon, also known as "Baby V," was born on March 18, 1984, in Baxley, Georgia, and raised in Fort Myers, Florida. Before appearing on *American Idol*, Vonzell worked as a postal carrier, though she also performed with local bands. She originally auditioned for *Idol* during season two, but didn't make the cut. In 2005, she finished third and was voted off on May 18.

Following her time on the show, Vonzell started her own record label, Melodic Records. On January 9, 2007, Vonzell (as Baby V) released an eight-song collection entitled *My Struggle* via the iTunes download service. She also appeared in the 2007 movie *Still Green* and has become a spokesperson for the United States Postal Service. Vonzell also recently performed in a production of *The Wizard of Oz* and toured with *Simply Ballroom*.

#4

Anthony Federov is a Ukrainian singer, born Anatoliy Vladimirovich Fedorov in the city of Yalta on May 4, 1985. He and his family came to America in 1994. Despite doubts that he would ever speak again following a childhood tracheotomy, Anthony became an excellent singer and a fourth season *American Idol* finalist. He was voted off on May 11, 2005, and finished in fourth place.

Anthony has yet to release his first CD, but is currently working on it. In June 2006, he was the runner-up in a special reality television version of *Fear Factor*. That September, he lost his brother to sarcoma (a type of cancer). As a result, he would go on to become a spokesman for the Sarcoma Foundation of America. Anthony also performed at the BMI Latin Music Awards in March 2009.

#5

Scott Thomas Savol was born in Cleveland, Ohio, on April 30, 1976, and moved along with his family to nearby Shaker Heights when he was 10. He was eliminated from *American Idol* on May 4, 2005, finishing in fifth place. Scott was, as the Musical Ramblings Web site put it, "the big guy with the R&B tenor voice that just came out of nowhere."

Scott has since returned to Cleveland, where he currently lives with his wife, Rachel, and son, Brandon. Now 33 years old, the musical everyman has a Christmas-themed song, "Upon a Christmas Night," available for download from his official Web site. He recently portrayed the Cowardly Lion in a Texas-based production of *The Wizard of Oz*, and was one of the headliners at the June 2008 "America's Favorite Finalists" concert.

#6

Constantine James Maroulis was born in Brooklyn, New York, on September 17, 1975, but grew up in Wyckoff, New Jersey. In 2002, he received a bachelor's degree in musical theater from the Boston Conservatory of Music. Constantine had performed theater and voice-acting work prior to his sixth-place finish on *American Idol*. He was eliminated on April 27, 2005.

Constantine's first album came with the rock band Pray for the Soul of Betty in 2005. He recorded "Bohemian Rhapsody," a song he performed on *Idol*, for a 2005 Queen tribute CD. Later he formed his own record label, Sixth Place Productions, and released his first solo album, *Constantine*, on August 7, 2007. He recently starred in the Broadway play *Rock of Ages*, and on May 5, 2009, received a Tony Award nomination for his work.

#7

Anwar Farid Robinson was born on April 21, 1979, in Newark, New Jersey. He trained as a tenor at Westminster Choir College in Princeton, New Jersey, and auditioned for *American Idol* in August 2004 in Washington, D.C. Anwar wound up in seventh place during season four, and was eliminated from the show on April 20, 2005, one day after his performance of "September" by Earth, Wind, and Fire.

Unlike most other *Idol* finalists, Anwar did not immediately pursue a record deal. Instead, he returned to New Jersey, where he became involved with the United Way and served as the co-chairman for a local literacy program. He completed two digitally distributed collections of cover songs, and is currently working on a CD of original music. Anwar also recently appeared in stage productions of the musicals *Rent* and *Godspell.*

#8

Nadia C. Turner was born in Miami, Florida, on January 11, 1977, and was named in honor of Olympic gymnast Nadia Comaneci. During her time on *American Idol,* she performed a show-stopping version of Dusty Springfield's "You Don't Have to Say You Love Me," as well as hits from Paul McCartney and Cyndi Lauper. Nadia was eliminated on April 13, 2005, finishing in eighth place.

This former Miami Dolphins cheerleader would later return to sing the national anthem prior to one of the NFL team's games. She has since performed at numerous charity events, and also appeared in the 2007 movie *Lord Help Us.* Nadia's first single, "Standing on Love," was released in 2008 as part of a promotion with Edy's Slow Churned Ice Cream. She is still at work on her debut CD.

#9

Osborne Earl "Nikko" Smith, Jr., the son of Baseball Hall of Famer Ozzie Smith, was born on April 28, 1982, and hails from St. Louis, Missouri. He was eliminated from *American Idol* not once, but twice—first on March 9, 2005, and then again on April 6 after being chosen to replace another contestant who quit the show. "The Comeback Kid" finished ninth.

Following his time on *Idol,* Nikko formed his own publishing label, the N Music Group, and immediately signed a trio of acts: D-Miles, Kane, and Alanna. On October 26, 2006, he performed the national anthem prior to Game 4 of the World Series in St. Louis, where his dad had played for 15 seasons. On September 1, 2008, he released *Revolution,* a collection of eight songs made available for download from online retailers.

#10

Jessica Ann Sierra was born in Tampa, Florida, on November 11, 1985. She had previously been a contestant on *Star Search* before becoming an *American Idol* finalist. Jessica was best known for her performance of the Bonnie Tyler song "Total Eclipse of the Heart." However, she wound up being the third finalist voted off, exiting the show on March 30, 2005.

After joining other fourth-season finalists on a 44-city tour, Jessica released her first single, "Unbroken," as part of a promotion with Sony and Toys R Us. On January 8, 2008, she released an eight-song EP for digital download. That EP, *Deepest Secret,* was later sold in CD format through her official Web site. Jessica has also had a well-publicized battle with substance abuse, but as of April 2009, she had been sober for about 18 months.

#11

Mikalah Analise Gordon was born in Las Vegas, Nevada, on January 14, 1988. From the ages of six to fourteen, she trained with Helen Joy Young Entertainers, and even performed at the White House. During *American Idol,* Mikalah was the second finalist eliminated, as she was voted off during *Billboard* #1 Hits week on March 24, 2005.

She has been immensely active since then. As an actress, Mikalah appeared on *Living With Fran* and *The Unit.* She hosted the Fox reality show *American Idol Extra* for two seasons and has worked as a correspondent for *The Tyra Banks Show.* In late 2008, she competed on the second season of the CMT show *Gone Country.* Mikalah is currently in the process of writing and recording her first CD. No release date has been announced.

#12

Lindsey Michelle Cardinale was born on February 5, 1985, in Hammond, Louisiana, but moved along with her family to nearby Ponchatoula at the age of six. At the age of 19, she went to New Orleans for *American Idol* auditions, making the cut and becoming friends with fellow contestant Carrie Underwood. On March 16, 2005, following a performance of "Knock on Wood," Lindsey became the first finalist eliminated.

After *American Idol,* Lindsey returned to her roots. She has become a regular performer at her hometown's annual Strawberry Festival, and is the spokesperson for an area car dealership. She has also released a maxi single featuring the songs "Drive" and "Nothin' Like a Dream," and recorded "Away in a Manger" for the *American Christmas* CD. In the summer of 2009, Lindsey staged concerts in North Carolina, Virginia, and Pennsylvania.

Although Taylor Hicks was the winner, season five's most successful finalists were nonwinners. Fourth-place Chris Daughtry's self-titled debut album sold a million copies in just five weeks, becoming the fast-selling debut rock album in history. Judge Simon later commented on the effect of Chris's success on later contestants by calling it "Chris Daughtry–itis"—a belief that competitors can be successful simply by making it into the top 10.

American Idol
Season

Starting with its fifth season debut on January 17, 2006, *American Idol* was broadcast in high definition for the first time. In many ways, season five was the most successful to date. Nine of the top ten and a total of seventeen contestants were able to secure record deals. Also, the May 24, 2006, finale, which saw Taylor Hicks beat Katharine McPhee, attracted an audience of more than 36 million people and was the highest rated final episode in series history. A total of 580 million viewers tuned in during the fifth season of *American Idol.*

#1

Taylor Reuben Hicks was born on October 7, 1976, in Birmingham, Alabama. He was an accomplished musician prior to *American Idol,* and had released a pair of independent CDs, *In Your Time* and *Under the Radar.* On May 24, 2006, thanks to a devoted group of fans known as the "Soul Patrol," Taylor was named the fifth season champion. He is the oldest *American Idol* winner of all time.

Taylor's popularity exploded after his win. He was named *People* magazine's Hottest Bachelor of 2006, and his June 13, 2006, debut single, "Do I Make You Proud?" debuted at the top of the *Billboard* charts. That December, he released a self-titled CD on Arista Records, and followed it up with a 2008 compilation of his early works. Taylor's most recent album, *The Distance,* hit stores on March 10, 2009.

#2

Katharine Hope McPhee was born in Los Angeles, California, on March 25, 1984. She spent three semesters studying musical theater at the Boston Conservatory, and was persuaded by then boyfriend/current husband Nick to try out for *American Idol.* Despite forgetting the words to "I Can't Help Myself" during the second round, she became a finalist and, on May 24, 2006, finished as the season five runner-up.

Katharine followed up her *Idol* success by performing with opera tenor Andrea Bocelli and playing the *J.C. Penney Jam: Concert for America's Kids* in June 2006. Her self-titled debut album was released on January 30, 2007, and has sold over 350,000 copies to date. Katharine has also pursued a career in acting and has recorded songs for various film soundtracks. Her second studio CD is due out in late 2009.

#3 **Efraym Elliott Yamin** was born in Los Angeles, California, on July 20, 1978. At the age of 16, he was diagnosed with Type I diabetes. Elliott's performance on *American Idol* drew praise from guest judge Stevie Wonder, who told the contestant that he should definitely become a professional musician. Elliott was eliminated by the smallest of margins on May 17, 2006, finishing in third place.

Elliott became one of the more prolific season five contestants. In 2006, he sang the national anthem at the NBA Finals and performed at the Virginia State Fair. He has released four total CDs: *Elliott Yamin* (2007), *Sounds of the Season: The Elliott Yamin Holiday Collection* (2007), *My Kind of Holiday* (2008), and *Fight For Love* (2009). Elliott has also been actively involved with the Juvenile Diabetes Research Foundation.

#4 **Christopher Adam "Chris" Daughtry** was born in Roanoke Rapids, North Carolina, on December 26, 1979. His performance of the Fuel song "Hemorrhage (In My Hands)" on the March 1, 2006, episode of *American Idol* was reportedly so good that the band extended an offer for Chris to become their lead singer. He declined and remained on the show, finishing fourth after being voted off on May 10.

In 2006, he formed the band Daughtry, which released their self-titled debut CD later that year. It sold more than four million copies, becoming the fastest selling rock music debut in history. In 2007, they were nominated for multiple Grammy and American Music Awards. Chris has also collaborated with other famous bands, including Live and Third Day. Daughtry's next album, *Leave This Town,* was released on July 14, 2009.

#5

Paris Ana'is Bennett was born in Rockford, Illinois, on August 21, 1988. She originally planned to go to medical school, but her grandfather convinced her to audition for *American Idol* instead. She vowed to leave the music business if she was rejected, but after strong performances of the songs "Take Five" and "Fever," she cracked the top five. Paris was eliminated fifth overall on May 3, 2006.

After being voted off the show, Paris contributed songs to the *American Idol Season 5: Encores* CD and the *Everyone's Hero* soundtrack. She performed at the 2006 Divas Simply Singing AIDS benefit concerts, released her first album, *Princess P*, on May 8, 2007. Paris followed that up with a 2008 collection of holiday songs, *A Royal Christmas*, and is expected to release her second studio album in late 2009.

#6

Kellie Dawn Pickler was born on June 28, 1986, in Albemarle, North Carolina. The 19-year-old had drawn comparisons to previous *American Idol* winner Carrie Underwood and pop sensation Jessica Simpson during her time on the show. She was voted off on April 26, 2006, following a performance of the Righteous Brothers' "Unchained Melody," and was the sixth-place finisher during season five.

Her first CD, *Small Town Girl*, was released on October 31, 2006, and became an instant hit, debuting atop the *Billboard* country charts and earning her Academy of Country Music and CMT Music Award nominations. Kellie also was honored for her work as a songwriter on the album. Her self-titled second CD followed on September 30, 2008, and in April 2009, she went on tour as the opening act for Taylor Swift.

#7 **Brett Asa "Ace" Young** was born in Denver, Colorado, on November 15, 1980. Prior to his time on *American Idol,* Ace's song "Reason I Live" had already been featured as part of *The Little Vampire* soundtrack. On April 4, 2006, his performance of Kenny Rogers's "Tonight I Wanna Cry" on the show earned kudos from Rogers himself. Ace finished seventh and was eliminated on April 19.

In October 2006, Ace released his first post-*Idol* single, "Scattered," on iTunes. Later that year, he performed during the Walt Disney Christmas Day Parade. In January 2008, Ace was named a Celebrity Ambassador for the Muscular Dystrophy Association, and his self-titled debut CD was released on July 15. He has also acted on the Fox TV show *Bones,* and recently made his Broadway debut in the musical *Grease.*

#8 **William Joel "Bucky" Covington III** is a Rockingham, North Carolina, native who was born on November 8, 1977. Both Bucky and his twin brother Rocky tried out for *American Idol,* but it was Bucky, a self-taught guitar player, who made it into the final 12. He was the fifth finalist to be voted off the show and was eliminated on April 12, 2006.

In November and December of that year, he performed as part of the GAC Country Music Christmas tour. Bucky's self-titled debut CD was released on April 17, 2007, and debuted atop the country music charts. In early 2009, he returned to the studio and began work on a second album, which was due out that September. He also made a cameo appearance in the 2009 motion picture *Hannah Montana: The Movie.*

#9

Mandisa Lynn Hundley was born on October 2, 1976, in Citrus Heights, California. Prior to *American Idol,* she earned a bachelor of music degree with a focus on vocal performance from Tennessee's Fisk University. Among her noteworthy performances on the show were "I'm Every Woman" and "I Don't Hurt Anymore." She was eliminated on April 5, 2006, and finished in ninth position.

With the release of her first CD, *True Beauty,* on July 31, 2007, Mandisa established herself as a bestselling Christian artist. The album debuted atop the Christian music sales charts and earned her Grammy and Dove Award nominations. She is also the author of the book *IdolEyes* and has contributed songs to *WOW Hits 2008* and *The Pirates Who Don't Do Anything* soundtrack. Her latest album, *Freedom,* hit stores on March 24, 2009.

#10

Lisa Gabrielle Tucker was born on June 13, 1989, in Anaheim, California. As a youth, she played Young Nala is the stage production of Disney's *The Lion King* and was a runner-up on *Star Search.* She was a senior in high school during the fifth season of *American Idol,* finishing in 10th place when she was eliminated on March 29, 2006.

Afterwards, Lisa graduated from high school, and made several appearances in the Anaheim area. She performed a duet with Dionne Warwick on the singer's 2006 album *My Friends & Me.* Lisa has also pursued a career as an actress, appearing in television shows such as *The Game, 90210, Zoey 101,* and *Born in the U.S.A,* and also played the role of Keisha in the 2009 motion picture *The Hustle.*

#11

Kevin Patrick Covais was born in Levittown, New York, on May 30, 1989. Like fellow finalist Elliott Yamin, Kevin is a Type I diabetic, and was a junior in high school during season five of *American Idol*. Despite winning praises for his performance of "When I Fall in Love" on March 21, 2006, he was eliminated the very next day and finished in 11th place.

Kevin returned to high school following *American Idol* and graduated in 2007. He has yet to sign a record deal but has pursued a career in acting. Kevin appeared in the movie *College* opposite Drake Bell, earned a guest-starring role on the CBS program *The Ghost Whisperer*, and played Greg in the 2009 romantic comedy *Labor Pains*. In addition, Kevin currently serves as a Youth Ambassador for the American Diabetes Association.

#12

Melissa Christine McGhee was born on September 14, 1984, in Tampa, Florida. She had originally auditioned during season two of *American Idol* but didn't become a finalist until the show's fifth year. However, she was the first finalist sent home. Melissa was voted off on March 15, 2006—one day after struggling with the lyrics to Stevie Wonder's "Lately" while the Motown great himself looked on.

Following *Idol*, Melissa performed at a few shows before undergoing vocal cord surgery and taking time off to recover. Once healthy, the 24-year-old singer further delayed work on her first CD so she could, according to her official MySpace page, "find out who I am as an artist." Melissa has since started recording material, and originally planned to tour during Spring 2009. That tour was later postponed, however.

After a record 74 million votes during the season six finale, Jordin Sparks was declared the winner over Blake Lewis. Many, including Simon, had believed that Melinda Doolittle was the most promising finalist, but she was voted off in third place. However, the season's most talked about contestant was seventh-place Sanjaya Malakar, who survived week after week with his constant, warm smile.

American Idol
Season

During the 2007 season, an average of 37 million viewers watched each episode of *American Idol*—the highest per episode total in series history. On January 16 and 17, things kicked off with back-to-back two-hour specials, and a two-hour finale aired on May 23. Season six also saw the debut of the *Idol Gives Back* charity event and the *American Idol* Songwriter Contest. Over 25,000 entries were received, and the winning song, "This Is My Now" by Jeff Peabody and Scott Krippayne, was recorded by sixth season champ Jordin Sparks.

#1

Jordin Brianna Sparks, daughter of former NFL player Phillippi Sparks, was born in Phoenix, Arizona, on December 22, 1989. Thanks to the support of her loyal fans, the "Sparkplugs," Jordin did not finish in the bottom three once and was never in danger of elimination. On May 23, 2007, the 17-year-old singer held off Blake Lewis to become the youngest winner in *American Idol* history.

Jordin's self-titled debut CD came out on November 20, 2007. Not only did it go platinum, but it also won her the NAACP Image Award for Outstanding New Artist. She went on to sing the national anthem at Super Bowl XLII, becoming the youngest person ever to do so. Also, in January 2009, she performed at President Barack Obama's Inaugural Ball. Jordin's next album is due out on July 14, 2009.

#2

Blake Colin Lewis was born on July 21, 1981, in Redmond, Washington. His unique version of the Bon Jovi song "You Give Love a Bad Name" was voted as one of the 20 greatest *American Idol* performances of all time by AOL.com. Blake made it all the way to the May 23, 2007 finale, where he lost to Jordin Sparks and finished as the season six runner-up.

On August 24, 2007, Blake signed with Arista Records, and his debut album, *A.D.D. (Audio Day Dream)* came out on December 4. The CD features a variety of different musical styles, leading Blake to refer to it as "electro-funk-soul-pop" during an interview with *TV Guide*. It peaked at number two on the *Billboard* album chart. Blake is currently recording material for an upcoming, currently untitled second CD.

3

Melinda Marie Doolittle, a former back-up singer for such performers as Alabama and Aaron Neville, was born in St. Louis, Missouri, on October 6, 1977. Her top *American Idol* performances included the songs "Sweet Sweet Baby (Since You've Been Gone)" by Aretha Franklin and "My Funny Valentine" by Frank Sinatra. Melinda finished in third place, and was voted off on May 16, 2007.

On June 12, 2007, Melinda released a self-titled, five-song compilation of cover songs, and on February 12, 2008, her performance of "My Funny Valentine" became available for digital download. Melinda's first full studio album, *Coming Back to You,* was released on February 3, 2009. In June 2009, she participated in the Challenge America benefit concert, and in July she played two shows in Japan as part of AmericaFest 2009.

4

LaKisha Ann Jones, who was born on January 13, 1980, in Flint, Michigan, was encouraged by her five-year-old daughter, Brionne, to try out for *American Idol*. She wowed judges during auditions with her performance of the Aretha Franklin song "Think," and became one of the 12 finalists. LaKisha was eliminated in fourth place on May 9, 2007.

Afterwards, LaKisha appeared on tour along with her fellow *American Idol* finalists, and received critical praise for her performance of "I Will Always Love You." She appeared as a voice coach on the TV show *Legally Blonde: The Search for Elle Woods*, and her first album, *So Glad I'm Me,* was released on May 19, 2009. She is currently married to financial advisor Larry Davis and is expecting her second child in August 2009.

#5

Christopher Michael Richardson was born in Belgium on February 19, 1984, and moved to Chesapeake, Virginia, in 1999. Chris had previously auditioned for *American Idol* twice before making the cut during season six. Despite drawing comparisons to Justin Timberlake by judge Randy Jackson, Chris was voted off in fifth place on May 2, 2007.

Chris became close friends with Blake Lewis during his time on *Idol* and joined the runner-up and the other sixth season finalists on tour following the finale. He has been at work on his debut album for several years, and in March 2008, he released a single from the album entitled "All Alone." He has also written songs for Lewis, Jordin Sparks, Phil Stacey, and others. Chris's CD, currently known as *All Alone,* is due out sometime in 2009.

#6

Joel Phillip "Phil" Stacey, the son of a nurse and a preacher, was born in Richmond, Kentucky on January 21, 1978. With his country music background, he shone during Country Week with his performance of "Where the Blacktop Ends" by Keith Urban. Phil was voted off along with Chris Richardson on May 2, 2007, officially finishing in sixth place.

Capitalizing on that success, Phil signed a recording deal with Lyric Street Records and released his self-titled debut album in April 2008. *Phil Stacey* was called "the best Nashville album from an *Idol* contestant who didn't win" by *USA Today*. He has since parted ways with Lyric Street Records, signing with Reunion Records in January 2009. Phil plans to release a collection of Christian music entitled *Into the Light* due August 25, 2009.

#7 **Sanjaya Joseph Malakar** was born on September 10, 1989, in Federal Way, Washington. Sanjaya was a fan favorite during his time on *American Idol*, and he could more than hold his own musically. Jennifer Lopez praised him following his performance of "Bésame Mucho," and Paula Abdul called him "charming" following his rendition of "Cheek to Cheek." Sanjaya was eliminated in seventh place on April 18, 2007.

Sanjaya was nominated for several fashion-related and television awards as a result of his time on *Idol*, and won the Teen Choice Award for Best TV Reality Star in 2007. He has released a half-dozen singles on iTunes to date, and in 2009, published a book about his experiences on the show. Sanjaya is set to compete in the upcoming NBC reality show *I'm a Celebrity . . . Get Me Out of Here!*

#8 **Haley Suzanne Scarnato**, who was born on June 15, 1982 in San Antonio, Texas, had spent much of her childhood as a gymnast before injuries led her to discover how much she enjoyed singing. The judges praised her voice during her time on *American Idol*. Nonetheless, Haley was eliminated in eighth place on April 11, 2007.

The San Antonio native has twice performed the national anthem prior to playoff basketball games featuring the hometown Spurs—once in 2007 and again on April 20, 2009. Haley also contributed the song "Have Yourself a Merry Little Christmas" for the *American Christmas* CD, and in April 2008, she released her first original single, "Girl's Night Out." In early 2009, she signed with Sands Entertainment, and her first album, *StrongHeart*, is due out before that year's end.

#9 **Gina Glocksen** was born on Independence Day, July 4, 1984, in Tinley Park, Illinois. Prior to her success during season six of *American Idol*, she had worked as a dental assistant and performed with a cover band on the side. She performed songs from The Supremes, The Rolling Stones, and The Pretenders, but was voted off in ninth place on April 4, 2007.

Gina participated in the post-season *American Idol* tour, and during one show, her fiancé, a fellow musician named Joe Ruzicka, surprised her on stage with a marriage proposal. They were married on New Year's Eve in 2008, with fellow *Idol* contestants Jordin Sparks and Haley Scarnato serving as bridesmaids. To date, she has recorded and digitally released four original singles, with "List of Regrets" being the most recent.

#10 **Charles Christopher "Chris" Sligh** was born in Greenville, South Carolina on July 20, 1978. During auditions, his performance of Seal's "Kiss from a Rose" earned him a standing ovation from Paula Abdul, and his unique personality definitely made him stand out from the crowd. Nonetheless, on March 28, 2007, Chris became the third finalist voted off.

Later on in 2007, he and his band, Half Past Forever, re-released their CD *Take a Chance on Something Beautiful*, and he participated in the *American Idol* tour. In May 2008, he released *Running Back to You*, a collection of Christian music that caused *USA Today* to label Chris "the most musically ambitious Idol to date." Since then, he has appeared on the 2008 Back to School Tour, the 2008 NewSong Christmas Celebration, and the 2009 Make It Matter Tour.

#11 **Stephanie Edwards**, who was born on November 5, 1987, in Savannah, Georgia, was a busy college freshman who nearly skipped the season six *American Idol* auditions. However, her parents insisted she audition, and she did, wowing the judges with her performances of Prince and Beyoncé songs and eventually earning her way into the top 12. Stephanie was eliminated in 11th place on March 21, 2007.

Stephanie has been somewhat quiet since her elimination from *American Idol.* In October 2007, she released a single called "On Our Way." The CD is available online, and proceeds from all sales benefit the Leukemia & Lymphoma Society's Light the Night Walk. In April 2008, she released a second single, "Here I Am," which was written by Julie Wilde and was an entry in the 2007 *American Idol* Songwriting Competition.

#12 **Brandon Rogers**, who was a professional backup singer before competing on *American Idol,* was born in Los Angeles, California, on December 11, 1977. He started performing at an early age, and was part of a choir that performed with Michael Jackson during halftime of Super Bowl XXVII. He was the first finalist eliminated from the show, finishing in 12th place on March 14, 2007.

While Brandon guest starred on the Fox television show *Bones* in May 2008, he remains committed to his music. In June 2008, he appeared as part of the America's Favorite Finalists concert in Branson, Missouri, and has also performed at numerous other venues throughout the years. Brandon's debut album, *Automatic,* was released by Authentik Artists on May 26, 2009. It is currently available through iTunes, Rhapsody, and other digital download services.

Season seven saw the second time two male finalists battled for the crown. Following in the footsteps of Bo Bice (season four) and Chris Daughtry (season five), David Cook became the first rocker to win the competition. The songwriter contest continued this season, and "The Time of My Life," written by Regie Hamm, was chosen from thousands of entries. David sang the tune as the winner's song during the season finale and later released it as his first single.

American Idol
Season

7

The seventh season of *American Idol* marked the first time contestants were allowed to use musical instruments. It debuted on January 15, 2008, ran through May 21, 2008, and drew an average of over 33 million viewers per episode. The finale pitted David Cook against David Archuleta. An *American Idol* record 97.5 million votes were received, with Cook earning 56 percent of the vote to defeat Archuleta. Also making its return was the *Idol Gives Back* special, which featured appearances by Brad Pitt, Bono, and Barack Obama, and raised more than $60 million for charity.

#1 **David Roland Cook** was born in Houston, Texas, on December 20, 1982. He originally only travelled to the show's auditions to support his younger brother, Andrew. However, Andrew talked David into trying out, and while Andrew himself did not make it to Hollywood, David became the seventh season winner on May 21, 2008.

The following week, David broke a *Billboard* record by having 11 of his songs debut on the Hot 100 chart. On November 18, 2008, he released his first CD since winning *Idol,* and the self-titled album sold over a million copies in the United States. David kicked off his first world tour in Tallahassee, Florida, on February 13, 2009. He is also involved with the Race for Hope–DC in memory of his older brother, Adam, who died of brain cancer in May 2009.

#2 **David James Archuleta** was born in Miami, Florida, on December 28, 1990. He was only 16 when he auditioned for *American Idol* but made it all the way to the finale. On May 21, 2008, even competitor David Cook praised his performances of "Don't Let the Sun Go Down on Me," "In This Moment," and "Imagine." Yet Archuleta finished as the seventh season runner-up.

In June 2008, David signed a deal with Jive Records and released his self-titled debut CD on November 11. *David Archuleta* was certified gold on January 29, 2009. He was named one of the Breakout Stars of 2008 by *Forbes* magazine and won two Teen Choice Awards. David made guest appearances on the popular teen shows *iCarly* and *Hannah Montana,* and in June 2009, he hit the road as the opening act for Demi Lovato.

#3

Syesha Raquel Mercado, the daughter of a former Motown back-up singer, was born on January 2, 2008, in Bridgeport, Connecticut. She auditioned in Florida, and after making it to Hollywood, temporarily lost her voice. However, she rebounded to perform a solid version of "Chain of Fools," in week three. Despite being in danger of elimination five times, Syesha lasted until May 14, 2008, and finished third.

Syesha participated in the American Idols Live! Tour following the end of the season, and appeared at the IKEA Thanksgiving Day Parade in Philadelphia, Pennsylvania. In December, she worked with Habitat For Humanity rebuilding houses in Miramar, Florida, and held a February 2009 concert with proceeds benefiting the Amer-I-Can program. Syesha also performed at the "Giving Hunger the Blues" show in April 2009, and is currently working on her first album.

#4

Jason René Castro is a Texas native, born in Dallas on March 25, 1987, and raised in the city of Rowlett. The Texas A&M student with his trademark dreadlocks was an early favorite in the competition, and even won an April 12 CNN fan poll. Jason played the ukulele on the show and sang in three languages, but was eliminated in fourth position on May 7, 2008.

During the finale of *American Idol*, he returned and performed the song "Hallelujah." It would go on to reach number one on the iTunes sales charts and was featured in the Mexican film *Amar a Morir*. In April 2009, Jason announced that he had signed with Atlantic Records and had written over 40 songs for an upcoming debut album. No release date for the CD has been announced.

#5

Brooke Elizabeth White was born on June 2, 1983, in Phoenix, Arizona, but grew up in nearby Mesa. In 2006, she recorded an independent CD entitled *Songs from the Attic,* which was later re-released. During season seven, the judges compared Brooke to a young Carly Simon or Carole King. She was voted off on April 30, 2008, and finished in fifth place.

Brooke immediately embarked on a media tour, appearing on such programs as *The Tonight Show with Jay Leno, Live with Regis and Kelly,* and *The Ellen DeGeneres Show.* She also participated in the American Idols Live! Tour through September 2008. In May 2009, Brooke launched her own record label, June Baby Records, and the singer-songwriter planned to release her next album, *High Hopes and Heart Break,* on July 21, 2009.

#6

Carly (Hennessy) Smithson was born in Dublin, Ireland, on September 12, 1983. She came to the U.S. to pursue a career in music at the age of 15, and in 2001 had released the CD *Ultimate High* for MCA Records. Despite the previous record deal, Carly became an *American Idol* finalist, and was eliminated in sixth place on April 23, 2008.

Following her elimination, she participated in the post-season tour along with the other members of the top 10, and performed the songs "Bring Me To Life" by Evanescence, "Crazy On You" by Heart, and "I Drove All Night" by Cyndi Lauper. Carly is recording material for an upcoming CD, which she says she will shop to record companies upon completion. In early 2009, she released "Let Me Fall," the first single from that album.

#7

Kristy Lee Cook was born in Seattle, Washington, on January 18, 1984. Kristy Lee had started performing in the late 1990s, and released her first CD, *Devoted,* in 2005. She sang "Amazing Grace" during her *American Idol* auditions, and battled through bronchitis during her first week in Hollywood. Kristy Lee was eliminated in seventh place on April 16, 2008.

Arista Nashville signed Kristy Lee on June 29, 2008, and released the single "15 Minutes of Shame" on August 12. Her first post-*Idol* CD, *Why Wait,* came out on September 16, and on October 25, she performed at the Grand Ole Opry for the first time. Since then, Kristy Lee has parted ways with Arista and is currently meeting with labels. She also keeps busy running the Kristy Lee Horse Heaven Foundation.

#8

Michael Johns was born Michael John Lee on October 20, 1978, in Perth, Western Australia. Michael moved to the U.S. in 1998 and found minor success with the band The Rising prior to his time on *American Idol.* An early performance of the Otis Redding song "I've Been Loving You Too Long" led judge Simon Cowell to note the soulful quality of his voice. He was voted off on April 10, 2008, finishing eighth.

On December 9, 2008, Michael released the song "Another Christmas," with proceeds from the sales of the single benefitting the Red Cross and the Muscular Dystrophy Association's ALS division. He also performed on and co-produced the soundtrack for the Shaun White documentary *Don't Look Down.* Michael's most recent CD, *Hold Back My Heart,* was released on June 23, 2009.

#9

Ramiele Macrohon Malubay was born to Filipino parents living in Dammam, Saudi Arabia on September 6, 1987. At four feet, eleven inches, she is believed to be the shortest contestant in *American Idol* history, and performed hits from The Beatles, Aretha Franklin, Phil Collins, and Dolly Parton during her time on the show. She was eliminated, in ninth place, on April 2, 2008.

The little *Idol* with the big voice, as the Associated Press dubbed her, completed the post–*American Idol* tour along with several other finalists over the summer of 2008. She has released several singles to date, including the songs "Kaya," "More to Me," and "Here I Am." The 2008 J.C. Penney Asian Excellence Award nominee is still pursuing a career in music, but also has plans to study optometry in the future.

#10

Chikezie Ndubuisi Eze was born on September 11, 1985, in Inglewood, California and is the son of Nigerian immigrants. Chikezie had previously made it to Hollywood during season six of *American Idol,* then returned for the seventh season and finished in 10th place. His final performance before exiting the show on March 26, 2008, was of the Luther Vandross song "If Only for One Night."

Following the post-season American Idols Live! 2008 concert tour, Chikezie has kept a fairly low profile. He is a former host of the TV Guide Network show *American Idols: Where Are They Now?* Also, he continues touring, appearing at El Camino Community College, his alma mater, on November 2, 2008. He has become a vegan, citing the health benefits of the lifestyle, and his debut album is due out sometime in 2009.

#11

Amanda Lindsay Overmyer was born in Little Rock, Arkansas, on October 26, 1984, and was raised in Camden, Indiana. Janis Joplin was one of Amanda's primary musical influences growing up, and ironically, during Amanda's time on *American Idol,* the judges actually compared her vocal style to that of the legendary singer. Amanda finished 11th overall and was voted off on March 19, 2008.

On May 24, 2008, just over two months after her elimination, Amanda headlined the Women of Rock concert in West Hollywood, California. That August, she played the Harley Davidson Summerfest in Milwaukee, Wisconsin. Amanda's first album, *Solidify,* was released for digital download on December 10, 2008. The southern-style rock CD, which features the single "Play On," was scheduled to hit stores sometime in 2009.

#12

David Anthony Hernandez was born on May 31, 1983, in Phoenix, Arizona, and was raised in nearby Glendale. He earned kudos from the judges for his performances of "Ain't Too Proud to Beg," "Papa Was a Rollin' Stone," and "It's All Coming Back to Me Now." David made the final 12, but was also the first member of the group eliminated on March 12, 2008.

Shortly thereafter, he performed at The Children's Hospital of New York Presbyterian, and on November 28, 2008, he embarked on a holiday tour along with fellow *American Idol* finalists Diana Degarmo, Kimberly Locke, and Chikezie. David also performed at the Declare Yourself Inaugural Ball in Washington, D.C. on January 18, 2009. He is currently working on his debut CD, which he hopes to have out before the end of 2009.

ABOUT THE AUTHOR

Chuck Bednar is an author and freelance writer from Ohio. He has been writing professionally since 1997 and has written more than 1,500 published nonfiction articles. Bednar is the author of more than a dozen books, including the *Tony Parker* and *Tim Duncan* entries in Mason Crest's MODERN ROLE MODELS series, as well as SUPERSTARS OF PRO FOOTBALL: *Tony Romo*. He is currently employed by Bright Hub (*www.brighthub.com*) as the Managing Editor for their Nintendo Wii Web site.